The Wandering Crane

Volume I

Feathers of Wisdom

By

Kevin Mooney

Library of Congress Control Number:
    2015901243

The Wandering Crane, Vol. I,
        "Feathers of Wisdom"
ISBN: 978-0-9885999-0-1

Published by:
        Leprechaun, Inc., North Port, FL

Cover Art:
        by Shawn Houser
Other Art
        by J. Bennett

Printed by A&A Printing, Tampa, FL. U.S.A.

Dedication

"The Wandering Crane series
        is dedicated
        to all the Beings
        I have encountered
        in the world
        of this world
        out of this world
        who allowed me
        to see
        into their souls
        to express
        my vision
        of their truth."

                                KM

Table of Contents

Frightened

With the forces of chaos
      whirling around

The drive to fantasy
      becomes acute

Crisis after crisis
      pushes us to security

But checking the forces
      we can't control

And taming the freedom
      of nature

We lose
      to chaos

Time to Fly

When the energy
>   of uncontrolled youth

Reaches the precipice
>   of manhood

A leap...
>   is made

That flies
>   at the face of death

A Note

Too many barriers

Too many barriers
    have been put in front
    of my path toward
    perfection

How many times
    can I bang my head
    against these walls

My head bleeds
    from the scars

The crown of thorns
    I cannot bear

I am not a noble hero
    a martyr
        to the cause of perfection

I am human

An animal
    that has been given a soul

Perfection exists
    somewhere

It is not my time
    to know where

I must believe
    I will have another chance

My life had to end
    as all lives do

But I must believe
    another time will come

for me

Another time
        to be the last

I pray

Going back and forth
        forever
        back and forth

I commit myself
        this time

But be back I will
        again

But not forever

I pray

Brothers

Within the bounds
      of worlds apart

A search is made
      that finds
      the same friend

The same hand
      to reach out
      and feel strong

Grief

In all its mortal moments
      there is no cure
      but time

Senseless death
      sees only light
      in God

A loneliness
      a barrenness
      fills the void

No fault of ours
      but humanity
      breeding souls
      that succumb
      to the vilest evil

But time cures
      and in this time
      time seems so slow

Revenge

An emotion
       that seems to come
       naturally
       until a realization
          is made
       that shadows
       the soul of man

What can be done
       can be forgiven
       in the wisest eyes
          of God

But we are not God
       and must abide
       by the rules
       of the universe
       not known
          til death

Dudley

To see your potential
  through another's eyes
  is enlightening

To know their potential
  through your eyes
  is wonderful

And to understand
  we see Christ
  through each others' eyes
  is glorious

Angels

Spirits that touch
     in a knowing way
     tread uneasily
     when separate
     from the truth

Warily they continue to touch
     and stop
     afraid of expectations
     not known
     not asked

Laving wonder
     and abandonment
     to sort out
     the interconnected energy
     of the universal synapses
     that fire the power of love

Marriage II

Two strong streams
      Unite
      to form a raging river
      that carves a path
      to the open sea
      together

Barriers

Space and time
      are but illusionary
      barriers
      manifesting fear
      of oneness

Jennifer

She is a light in the sky
        a star

She has the fire of love
        to melt
        even the coldest
        hearts

She has the determination
        of a comet
        to travel
        the universe
        unafraid
        of the slightest
        debris

But Jennifer does not see

From her perch
        high in the heavens
        she looks out

and sees
only darkness
loneliness
hopelessness

She sees a far off star
so pretty
in the night
glittering
twinkling
burning

She wonders why
that can't be her

Why is it
she sees
only desolation

Why is it
she is trapped
from all she sees

Who can tell her

she is
what she sees

She is that shining star
burning so bright

Who can tell
this stubborn star
to step back
and see the frame
around the mirror

Not I

I am hidden
behind the mirror
I hold
in my tired hands

Knowing You

It is easy to know you
in an instant
of truth
that challenges me
to learn
the expressions
you choose
as you walk your path
through walls
of fear
I laugh
I smile
I cry

Love Is

Love does not change
        it neither grows
        nor does it fade away

We only open
        or close
        our eyes
        to what love
        really is

Gone Away

Going away parties
    are supposed to be fun

Going away parties
    are supposed to be sad

Going away parties
    are supposed to be filled
    with hope

But who said you could go away?

And who said I could not?

So you be sure
    to have the pillow fluffed

And you be sure
    to have the bed all warm

For I'll be seeing you
soon enough

Because I love you

A Candle

When I left home
        so long ago
        to travel
        the adventurous avenues

I placed in my window
        a candle
        so small
        to lead me home
        when all was done

And on the road
        I sometimes looked
        back to see
        the light of home
        only to find
        no sign of peace

But though my heart
        did try to trust
        and try to believe

all was well

The dark cloud of doubt
     tried to hide
     the knowledge
     I could not forget

For when it was time
     to rest at home
     I saw the light
     oh, so small
     but strong
     leading me home
     to peace

Wind and Rain

The wind slowly blows
      away the
      extraneous particles
      of decay
      just as the rain
      diligently washes
      and cleanses
      the hardened stone

But if the wind and the rain
      invade my life
      I put an army
      on the march
      to block the rain
      and hold back the wind

I will build a fortress
      to fight the forces
      that direct my change

But even as the wind and rain

slowly wears away
the mightiest stone
so will change
correct my path
and clean my windows
for a wiser view

But even if I succumb
to windows washed clean
I do not have to see

The Reluctant Healer

For years he hides away
      neither wanting
      nor taking
      responsibility
      for the spirit within
      guiding him
      to his fulfillment

He searches for happiness
      in any other place
      but where he knows
      it is waiting

Trying desperately
      to find
      a different road
      a less demanding road
      a less courageous road
      in the minds of men

But all his roads
        end in dead ends
        that only turn him
        around
        back toward the road
        he fears the most

To learn
        fear is unnatural
        happiness awaits
        and fulfillment is his
        in the place
        most will not recognize
        as reality

A Private Ritual

Sit at ease
        be quiet for awhile

Bathe in the white golden light
        of your inner spirit
        to reconnect
        with the universal God
        and remember
        reality

Relax and breathe
        the healing green light
        as it sifts through the body
        purifying
        your communication tool

Let your body breathe
        with pure creative energy

Release the impurities
        through the pores

of your skin
as sweat
and salt
move them along
to cleanse
the entire body

Shower in the white golden light
and dry yourself
with a warm towel
of pink

The color of unconditional love

Awake refreshed
cleansed
energized
with a little memory
of home

Bump in the Night

In waking moments
      we are great friends
      who play
      and laugh
      and sing

In waking moments
      we stategize
      and take respite
      from sleep

For when we sleep
      we separate
      and go our paths
      alone

Learning
      and living
      and loving
      and growing

with those who need us
   most

And in this sleep
   on lonely paths
   we play a game
   of 'Hide and Seek'
   to keep us having fun

We change ourselves
   the best we can
   and try to find
   the other out

Looking high
   looking low
   sometimes close
   sometimes found
   sometimes not

But always
   there's the game

Just like kids
        in schoolyard play
        breaking up the time

For when we wake
        and talk
        and laugh
        we tell the tales
        of who found who
        inside the deepest sleep

And sometimes
        neither one has seen
        the other
        even close

But once upon an age of time
        it happens
        once or twice

We find each other
        in the night
        quite simply
        like a bump

Mathew 6: 25-34

I warn you then
       do not worry
       about your livelihood
       what you eat
       or drink
       or use for clothing

Is life not more than clothes?

Look at the birds in the sky
       they do not sow
       or reap
       they gather nothing
       into barns
       yet your heavenly Father
       feeds them

Are you not more important
       then they?

Which of you
       by worrying
       can add a moment
       to his lifespan?

Learn a lesson
       from the way
       the wild flowers grow

They do not work
       they do not spin
       yet I assure you
       not even Solomon
       in all his splendor
       was arrayed
       like one of these

If God can clothe
       in such splendor
       the grass of the field
       which blooms today
       and is thrown on the fire
       tomorrow
       will He not provide

much more for you?

Oh weak of faith!

Stop worrying then
over questions like
"What are we to eat?"
or
"What are we to wear?"

The unbelievers
are always running
after these things

Your heavenly Father
knows all
that you need

Seek first His Kingship
over you
His way of holiness
and all things
will be given you
besides

Enough then of worrying
about tomorrow
let tomorrow
take care of itself
today has enough troubles
of its own

Sorcerer's Apprentice

When the sorcerer's apprentice
        learns to bring the rain
        to the parched fields
        of his people
        he may be overjoyed
        but must also remember
        he is no master
        until he knows
        when not to bring the rain

Into the World

A long time ago
  and yet
  in the blink of an eye
  you went on a mission
  a mission for God

At that time
  there was trepidation
  knowing
  you would lose sight
  of home
  lose the certainty
  that home
  was even there

But you went
  into the world
  to do God's bidding
  and in that world
  you struggled
  and learned

the ways
of the children of God
who forgot to laugh
when they had
the mad idea
they could be separate
from God

At times
you felt abandoned
unloved
alone
but you were pushed
forward
and finally reached
those you needed to reach

Even then
it felt the struggle
would not end
but you wisely realized
you did not just teach
but learned as well

You came to be
       at home in the world

A world
       finally comfortable

But when
       the learning is done
       and the teaching
       at an end
       it is time
       to come home
       where the candle
       has burned
       so you would not forget

And do not think
       those you leave behind
       will not be as close
       as they are now
       for all the children of God
       are one
       and cannot be separated

You will see
>   the laughter in that
>   when you come back
>   home

Take your time
>   but do not tarry
>   a great feast is prepared.
>   for your homecoming

Housecleaning

Open
> the windows
> and let
> the fresh breeze
> cast away
> the cobwebs

Find
> the doors
> and fling
> them open
> too

Smell
> what's in the air
> and see
> what you can find

Let
> the mind float
> and careen

with all the ideas
and fears
and hopes

Let

the emotions
flood
to the rooftop
while you float
above it all
discerning
what is true

Amid

the once
shuttered house
you will find
your soul

Do not

be afraid
but overjoyed

The Search for Unconditional Love

I came here a long time ago
> looking for adventure
> and remembering
> the unity
> of life and love

I came here a long time ago
> sure of the love
> we all shared
> for each other

I came here a long time ago
> thinking
> the world understood
> unconditional love

But as I grew
> and was nurtured

into this body
into this society
I was distracted

The ecstasy of the body
enchanted me
enveloped me
until I forgot
I was in this world
and not of this world

In my sensual pleasure
of learning
about this world
I became enamored
of the rules
and regulations
that others created
without thinking
of the consequences

I enjoyed the touch
 the smell
 the sights
 the sounds
 the tastes of life
 that distracted me
 so much

I fell in love with life
 this wonderful place
 where senses
 were activated
 which were never
 touched before

I did not have these senses
 before
 and did not know
 there were
 consequences

I was overjoyed
     and intoxicated
     from childhood

I was addicted
     to the sensual experience
     presented to me

I took the guidelines
     offered to me
     as the easy road
     to pleasure

I did not care what was true
     only what was accepted
     so I could be sure
     to continue my joy
     of life
     with no responsibility

My life was taught
        to continue
        what was taught
        before
        without question
        so that we may continue
        to enjoy life
        without stress
        without thought
        without decision

But on this road
        of carnal experience
        I found a level of life
        I could not ignore

A subtle acknowledgment
        of thought
        beyond pleasure
        beyond stability
        of pleasure

No longer was it necessary
   to enjoy
   the simple pleasures
   of life

No longer was it enough
   to follow the rules
   written so many years ago

These rules were written
   when the first pioneers
   came to this place
   to explore

They had reason
   to maintain
   a sense of stability
   as we grew accustomed
   to this world
   this body

A necessary step
       as we evolved
       and understood our place
       our world
       our universe

And now it is time
       to look beyond
       the brave pioneers
       who paved the way
       who broke the rules
       who entered this life
       unaccompanied

Now is the time
       to search the annals
       to find the beginnings
       of thought
       that understood love
       from the most basic
       unconditional perspective

We have been so entranced
    in the body
    in this world
    that we forgot
    we are not of this world
    but are spirits
    that love beyond bodies

There is no body
    we love
    only spirit
    we understand
    as the soul of our brother
    and there is no separation
    from love of that being

How do we overcome
    the fear of the staus quo
    of the body
    of the world
    so that we remember

the love of the spirit
which does not include
the body
the world
but only the spirit
the soul

You must remember
you cannot love
another being
more or less
than another
you can only decide
to be more or less
intimate
with that being

Always remember
you are in the world
and not of the world

INDEX